# My First Portuguese
## Alphabets

---

**Picture Book with English Translations**

Published By: MyFirstPictureBook.com

# Aa

## Avião

Airplane

# Bb

## Bola

Ball

# Cc

## Casa

Home

# Dd

Dedo

Finger

# Ee

## Elefante

Elephant

# Ff

## Flor

Flower

# Gg

## Gato

Cat

# Hh

# Helicóptero

## Helicopter

# Ii

## Inseto

Insect

# Jj

## Janela

### Window

# Kk

## Karatê

Karate

# L l

## Livro

Book

# Mm

## Maçã

Apple

# Nn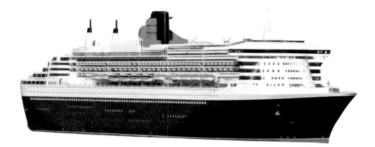

## Navio

Ship

# Oo

## Olho

Eye

# P p

## Pão

Bread

# Qq

## Queijo

Cheese

# Rr

## Relógio

### Clock

# Ss

## Sino

Bell

# Tt

## Tigre

Tiger

# Uu

## Uva

Grape

# Vv

## Vaca

Cow

# Ww

**W**indsurf

Windsurfing

# Xx

## Xícara

Cup

# Yy

Yoga

Yoga

# Zz

# Raiz

## Root

Made in the USA
Middletown, DE
22 February 2022